D1797866

I Am Not Trying to Hide My Hungers from the World

I Am Not Trying to Hide
My Hungers from the World

poems by

Kendra DeColo

American Poets Continuum Series, No. 185

BOA Editions, Ltd. ❖ Rochester, NY ❖ 2021

Copyright © 2021 by Kendra DeColo
All rights reserved
Manufactured in the United States of America

First Edition
21 22 23 24 7 6 5 4 3 2 1

For information about permission to reuse any material from this book, please contact The Permissions Company at www.permissionscompany.com or e-mail permdude@ gmail.com.

Publications by BOA Editions, Ltd.—a not-for-profit corporation under section 501 (c) (3) of the United States Internal Revenue Code—are made possible with funds from a variety of sources, including public funds from the Literature Program of the National Endowment for the Arts; the New York State Council on the Arts, a state agency; and the County of Monroe, NY. Private funding sources include the Max and Marian Farash Charitable Foundation; the Mary S. Mulligan Charitable Trust; the Rochester Area Community Foundation; the Ames-Amzalak Memorial Trust in memory of Henry Ames, Semon Amzalak, and Dan Amzalak; the LGBT Fund of Greater Rochester; and contributions from many individuals nationwide. See Colophon on page 104 for special individual acknowledgments.

NATIONAL ENDOWMENT for the ARTS
arts.gov

State of the Arts
NYSCA

Cover Design: Sandy Knight
Cover Art: Katherine Bradford (United States, born 1942), *Woman Flying*, 1999. Oil on canvas dropcloth, 84 x 72 inches. Portland Museum of Art, Maine. Museum purchase with support from the Friends of the Collection, 2012.14. Image courtesy of Pillar Digital Imaging.
Interior Design and Composition: Richard Foerster
BOA Logo: Mirko

BOA Editions books are available electronically through BookShare, an online distributor offering Large-Print, Braille, Multimedia Audio Book, and Dyslexic formats, as well as through e-readers that feature text to speech capabilities.

Library of Congress Cataloging-in-Publication Data

Names: DeColo, Kendra, author.
Title: I am not trying to hide my hungers from the world / poems by Kendra DeColo.
Description: First edition. | Rochester, NY : BOA Editions, Ltd, 2021. | Series: American poets continuum series; no. 185 | Summary: "Punk-rock feminist poems exploring motherhood, pop culture, and resistance with a spirit of defiance, abundance, and irreverent joy"— Provided by publisher.
Identifiers: LCCN 2020051906 (print) | LCCN 2020051907 (ebook) | ISBN 9781950774357 | ISBN 9781950774289 (ebook)
Subjects: LCGFT: Poetry.
Classification: LCC PS3604.E25 I26 2021 (print) | LCC PS3604.E25 (ebook) | DDC 813/.6—dc23
LC record available at https://lccn.loc.gov/2020051906
LC ebook record available at https://lccn.loc.gov/2020051907

BOA Editions, Ltd.
250 North Goodman Street, Suite 306
Rochester, NY 14607
www.boaeditions.org
A. Poulin, Jr., Founder (1938–1996)

Contents

For Elia and Avi

In memory of my grandmother, Mimi

and let the pleasure we invent together
be one more sign of freedom.

—Julio Cortázar

I Pump Milk like a Boss

I pump milk on the side of the road where the grass is biblical green
as if first cousin to the cow, her pink and swollen tits immaculate

as the plumbing of a church organ sending up calls to god, brassy mesh
of notes, fermented and dank as kush. I pump milk with my bare hands

into a bar's bathroom sink, above which is a mirror where someone's
    scrawled
I Love Cricket Pussy and below that, Everyone Deserves to be Loved.

I look at myself under the fingered smudge, the bodily fluids spattered
like haikus and I pump as if my milk is propaganda,

fingers bowing across my chest like a pawnshop violin,
milky graffiti tagging the spit-clogged drain.

I pump like I'm writing my name in blood
which turns to the milk my child sucks dry, which she turns into blood.

I pump like I have a tattoo on my pudenda
that says Aerosmith backwards, I pump

as if my hands have teeth, one combat boot hitched up on the toilet seat,
each hiss of milk chanting like a choir *yes bitch yes,*

my tits bitten and salt-veined, as when my baby
took her first gulp of air, humming

from the engorged crevasse of me
like a herd of wildebeest, as if the hive of me could have burst,

the infrared honey, the *glop glop*
of afterbirth dripping down my left leg,

spittle and amen, amniotic residue
fluorescent with prayer—

Do men lactate is a popular Google search and I wonder
what would happen if they could, our presidents

lifting their offspring to their breasts in the deep pockets
of night, listening to the dribble of milk

sipped from the pulpit of their bodies. Tonight my breasts
became so engorged I said I'd pay someone to suck my tits

half-joking. But a woman who heard followed me to the bathroom,
    read me
a sex poem while I pumped my milk, leaning away from the need in
    her voice

and the milk came slow and I pumped and waited for her to finish
and a streetlight scribbled in the parking lot

and I know there is a price we pay for loneliness
and a price we pay to forget it and I dedicate my libido

to my younger self and this is how I want to live, milk-stained, a little
    bit emptied,
a little bit in love with the abundance of my body,

my milk pale yellow with a layer of cream
which I will save long after it's turned, praising its curdled glow

every time I open the fridge, as if its presence is enough to keep me safe,
as if it's enough to make me invincible.

I Write Poems About Motherhood

Tonight I can write the most motherly lines,
for example: it's true, my asshole will never be the same

after giving birth, not its shape, but its soul, small wick
of shadow I once called *home* and *dream*. Tonight

I can write how it burned like a votive, the whole
inverted star a series of grievances from which another

self grew, séance and seam, split off
to live parallel lives like vaporish twins. I can write

that I gave birth and died and came back to life
and my asshole will never be the same. It wore

a haunted look those first few weeks. Claimed
it needed to "take fresh airs" in the country, wore

aggressively Victorian clothes and strutted
around naming geodes like a gentlemen

farmer. *Shut up, asshole,* I admonished. Tonight I write
my daughter emerged and split me into two selves. It did not hurt

the way they said it would. I rocked on my knees
singing a song like hurtling my voice off a cliff.

My husband's hand disappeared into mine
and for a moment I left this world, a hem of blood

between us. I broke onto the shore of a fixed
note. I helixed and drank the urine of starved

apparitions to keep me afloat, slapped the shit
out of my reflection, squatted and squeezed

a rocky planet out from the blue horizon
like a ship bifurcating a labial sky. But my asshole,

to whom I must now give credit where credit is due,
taught me how to anchor to the earth, locate the hot center

which I always knew was there but never saw
shining in my sacrum like Orion's belt

when they stitched me shut in a ragged,
casual way, even though I wished

to stay open a little longer,
unhinged and full of silences. Tonight I can write

that I would give birth a million times
over and not tell anyone about it

if I could feel that kind of way again:
one hollowed self opened wide

enough to swallow my own body
then spit it back out onto the earth.

*I Would Like to Tell the President to Eat a Dick
in a Non-Homophobic Way*

I would like for him to really taste the dick

Savor it like a last meal

Note the way it has or hasn't been recently washed

The residue of baby powder and sweat

Sheathed at the base like a foamy negligee

I'd like for him to choke on the dick

If that's what he's into and it's been talked about beforehand

I'd like for him to really get to know

The dick, how it curves to the left and bends towards justice

How it is sweet and bitter under the foreskin

How it is unashamed

Of its history

And knows where it's going

And while we're on the subject

I would like for Paul Ryan and Mitch McConnell to eat a bunch of
    dicks too

Casual, Lunchables-style dicks, a confetti

Of frosting-covered dicks exploding

In their taste buds like a Saturday morning balloon-drop

I would like to ask the president to eat so many dicks

That he vows to eat more pussy

Which have vitamins and minerals

And the secrets to success

Until he feels clean

Until he feels as close to the face of god as a man can get

Until he loves dick and pussy so much he shakes

Like a man redeemed in a church revival tent

Understanding that first there was the word and the word was

Let them eat dicks

And the word was good

Lord, let him eat a dick

That knows it will one day die

A dick that expects nothing in return

Humble dick

Tired dick

The dick he must eat

The one he has feared his whole life

The dick that might fill the endless void inside

Love Poem in the Style of Jordan's Furniture

Sometimes I sing New England furniture commercial jingles
to my husband so he might understand me better,

the ones where Boston accents reverberate
like moans in an empty church,

amniotic and relentless, sedating the ear
with elongated vowels like "COME ON

DOWN" and "I DOUBT IT," blunt
anthems we'd recite as kids

until some adult would scoff, "They can't learn
math but they can remember this" and today

while singing one of those songs
to my daughter before bed I felt so American

it hurt, like wandering pickle-deep
in the condiment aisles at Costco, half distracted

by someone asking what kind of meatball
I'd like while YouTube footage

of a Nazi getting punched in the face unfurls
across my phone's screen, his smirk

a sick apology, and I watch it again
beside the mayonnaise jars that are waiting to be snapped up

by doomsday preppers where they will glow
like engorged lanterns

in the basements of musty imaginations—
enough mayonnaise to last through the apocalypse,

not real nourishment but a temporary fix—
not real justice but close enough to feel

like I'm flashing my heart to everyone
in the superstore, asking them to hold it

for just a moment, place the fat joy
of it into their mouths,

the way I ask my husband to hold
this gilded bluster and sprawl

of a busted dialect, a language jagged
as rocks like odes to all of the things

I never learned, which might be the most
American thing about me,

loving what should make me feel ashamed,
filled with unimpeachable pride.

I Am Thinking About the Movie Con Air

I am thinking about the movie *Con Air* and my love
for Nicolas Cage, which is profound and focused

on the abundance of his hair, the way it trickles and recedes
to the middle of his scalp, chorusing down his back

with an unevenness that mirrors the body's swollen
inadequacies, one of my breasts

whistling with milk while the other sleeps
flat against my chest, the asymmetrical

splendor a speaker swelling with fuzz and odd
time signatures, like half of my body

restored to its original form. I never met Nicolas Cage
but watched *Con Air* so many times I can conjure

the chiaroscuro dribble of his voice, blue smoke
lapping the edge of an extinguished star,

and imagine he, too, knows how to disguise
the body into something less fragile,

the tired meat of his heart striated
into a thousand directions like a smoldering compass

as when I gave birth the midwives praised my composure,
said their last patient clawed the bed like a raccoon,

and I wished instead to have given birth like a squid
shooting an ombré cage of ink and ovum

out of her orifice, ragged and deranged
with hormones, because didn't I hold my daughter

and wish to be as feral as a raccoon
who knows love is the blunt metronome

of rummaging through trash, who doesn't
think but throws her body into the labor of it?

In the last scene Nicolas Cage grips the pink bunny
he bought from commissary,

ripped-up and dripping with fuel,
and hands it to his daughter anyway

and I will watch it over again
to see him stand there bruised and lit

with the one good thing he has;
my left breast emptied while the other

floods with music,
soothing the vowel-starred tongue.

Self-Portrait as Getting Drunk-Dialed by God

Oh to be shameless as a bachelorette party
singing "Friends in Low Places"

as they cruise 12 South
in a pedal tavern. Maybe it's the jealousy

in me that gives birth to the aftertaste
of defiance, whose flavor is not unlike blood,

not unlike a Bible opened
randomly to procure a message,

but what if the message is something
about vegetables or the perils of menstruation

or the proper way to wash one's hands?
Who am I kidding. I've never

read the Old Testament. I'm just a half Jew
who's never been Bat Mitzvahed

standing at an intersection in Nashville
where a flurry of blondes stake claim

to this city's malnourished heart,
where they chant Gucci Mane

and Brad Paisley lyrics and hitch
up their skirts like blessings,

a broken sort of dazzlement,
sun-soaked as the cleft of dunes

where I lost my virginity
(claimed my non-virginity?)

while my family picnicked nearby.
Dear God, if you are real,

I hope you have gold teeth
and watch *Game of Thrones*,

that you love the ice cream cone
gilded across Gucci's face

whose teeth were once beautiful
and profane as typewriter keys,

luxurious premonitions,
gold as the drag queen's eyelashes

who snorted a whole passage of cocaine
off my clavicle one night at the Grotta Bar,

gold as John Waters' aura and the blinking
rims of his bicycle, the only stranger

I've ever wanted to blow
for my own pleasure, a kind of devotion,

gold as the feeling I get when I'm lied to
out of mercy, the way I believe

you must lie to us sometimes,
those late night calls

where all I can hear is your heavy breathing
and you mumble

"I love you" just once
before hanging up.

Weaning, I Listen to Tyler, the Creator

sing about boredom, the edges
of my body punctured & rife

with gold as if his syntax
might blunt the crude untethering

that makes me monstrous,
my desire to be milkless flecked

with curled rinds of clementines
found behind the radiator

like little asphyxiated moons,
How much longer will there be music

in me? I believe sometimes
the government listens

to me & my husband fuck,
a census of every slop-induced

breath, each stitch in my rib
plucked to a glossy *amen.*

There is no simple way
to say I am ungovernable.

My daughter drinks & unearths
the heart underneath my heart,

feral & delicately ambushed
by the sun-smear of her breath,

my body no longer a love song
but a loudspeaker reverberating stolen time.

Weaning, I Listen to Paganini's Concerto No. 1

When I'm alone my tits scream
while the refrigerator

hums like a man nodding
off behind me on the bus.

There is never any food
I want to eat and I am ravenous

all the time: soft-boiled
eggs and mint tea. Milk

thick as leftover grease
stored under the sink.

My friend is a dairy farmer,
which means she delivers

cows, pulls velvety hooves
from gaping maws like psalms

into the muck and wet
hay. We haven't spoken

since my daughter was born
but maybe our friendship

ended when I was eight months
pregnant and she told me about

a stillbirth over the phone
how the mother

kept licking the calf's body
drowned in dull light

and I couldn't unhear
her voice, no matter how much

I believed it might unstitch
me from my own grief,

the way I became no more
or less beautiful

when I became a mother,
more like the perpetual

frost of astonishment
across a windshield,

more like I was doubled
and emptied, permanently

bent as if tending to a wound
or some unspeakable joy.

Why in Some Hospitals They Don't Let You
Hold Hands During Labor

Consider the perineum
stretched like cheap nylons

each night, two fingers
then three dipped in oil

opening the taint's
buttery seam. Consider

the bloody asterisk
of mucus plug,

amniotic sac
that refused to break

until I unhooked
from the saline drip

and danced until I pissed
myself, urine streaming pink

down my legs. Consider
the wedding band

my husband removed
before I crushed

his hand at ten centimeters,
bit his knuckle as if excavating

myself from a wreck;
excrement and buckets of ice,

the mirror someone placed
between my legs until I understood

I didn't need it, closed my eyes
and orchestrated my own

resurrection, cupping the dark
oil of my daughter's hair

as she emerged. Yes, I would have
pulled my husband into the abyss with me,

tearing open in every direction
like a star. I would have cracked

his carpals like a piano's brittle keys
like snapping the neck of a dove.

I would have burned the whole place down
to get where I needed to go.

Love Letter with The Beatles, Lana Del Rey, and Julio Cortázar

I feel most like a mother
at the coffee shop drinking decaf
and eating a Costco-brand
granola bar discreetly
wishing it had a different name
or something with Chia Seeds exuding
a nonchalant kind of wealth
when someone slides *Rubber Soul*
on the record player and I stop
what I'm doing because it is holy
to give this album your attention

Have you ever wanted to be so rich
your uterus is glitzed as a luxury apartment
lips Lana Del Rey swollen
lifting every song from the ether of glamour
and grief bee-stung
with a hunger that keeps us honest
so that we're bursting
with it sometimes the hydraulics
of ghosts jacked up on perverse longing?

The first song plays like a cigarette marquee
blinking subliminal commands
and I feel most like a mother
when I'm disappointed no one else
appears moved as if they've wrestled
their demons at 4 a.m.
a dervish of fast food wrappers
and tax returns
spilling from the back of a garbage truck
swishing through predawn

streets as when I would nurse my daughter
and a bloom of lochia unfurled
its salamander heart
beneath us

The record skips
like the synapse of recognition
when I first spotted you
across a field the feeling that says
I would explode right now
if I lingered too long
on the thought of you

I read a think piece on Lana Del Rey
tits thrumming with urgency
waiting to be pumped and wonder
if selling oneself is a kind of authenticity
or if ambition makes you less
honest I mean attractive
lord I am so tired

Most like a mother cataloging
stints of grief the singe and hiss
of a record making contact
like the wheels of a car
doing donuts in a parking lot
remembering the smell
of summer and rubber burning
my tits full of ash

Pompeii tits Burning Man tits
just graduated and touring Europe
tits my tits are not flashy
but comfortable living just within their means
happily married and paying taxes
on time tits sometimes unwashed

sometimes restless and wanting
to masturbate with nowhere to go
most like a mother when orgasms
are ashy apparitions my body
a phonograph leaking combustible notes
most like a mother wandering the aisles
of Costco the apples unholy and apoplectic
with polish whose skins
wince as I walk by tingling smugly
in the vegetable locker
like a morgue of refrigerated air

Most like a mother shaving my legs
in the bathroom at Wendy's
or not brushing my teeth most like a mother
on the playground
making small talk with other mothers and feeling
worn out and hollowed
among the rows of expensive strollers my inner tape deck ticking
I want to be rich I want to be rich I want to be rich
to win the contest of most motherly

fuck mothers fuck target fuck
listservs fuck nanny shares
fuck blogs fuck Ivanka fuck registries
fuck mother industrial complex
fuck Scary Mommy fuck permission
to eat frozen pizza alone and cry

If I hadn't met you
I'd probably be in an open "relationship"
with someone who wears a man bun
and says things at 38 like
I want children just not right away
who plays in a band and lets me pay his rent
who asks for ferret support
a year after we break up

I feel most like a mother
when I think of how lucky we are
and still resent
everything about you

Most like a mother
wanting to hide my big ass and thighs
wanting to celebrate my big ass and thighs
feeling it's an accomplishment
to go out in public and let myself
be seen most like a mother
when the young barista spills my drink
and calls me ma'am
and doesn't look at me

Most like a mother
shapeless in the bruised light
drenched in the pre-echo of another song
about to play wanting to steal every line
our daughter says and put it in this poem
"emphatic yogurt" and "the fox is holding
the moon"

I'm saying I love
the soft reception of your body

how the night she was born
you paced the room
singing Wreckless Eric
I'd go the whole wide world
I'd go the whole wide world

the dimmed fluorescence
of our singular heart
clanging *more more more*

How it rained
so hard one night in April
driving home from a cafe in Queens
where we'd eaten sweet tamales
I thought we might drown
but we didn't and I want to say
that was the night she was conceived
I want to say

Everything I'd want from you
is finally so little
because finally it's everything

Husk and sugar
an apartment filled with music
hiss of damp clothes
drying on the radiator,
a prayer made with a record's broken needle
to become beaming
and undone

How to Nurture Your Inner Life

1. Take long walks, gray hairs frizzled in the humidity, baby sleeping on your chest. 2. Nod as if listening to music. 3. Record the sound of falling chestnuts, the neighbor's Shih Tzus rushing the fence. 4. Pretend you're going somewhere important. 5. Tune out. 6. Let yourself look like a mess. 7. Ignore the neighbor. 8. Hold your own hand like you held your friend's hair while she puked up strawberries in your dorm bathroom, the tiles stained pink for weeks. 9. Remember the smell of your sister's wine vomit in the back of your Honda. You had a job interview the next day and got it even though you didn't want it. 10. Get hungry, get angry, feel like you're cornered and your cut man has disappeared. 11. Do not nap. 12. Send angry emails. 13. Tend to your jealousies like a mother of dragons. They will protect you when you need them. 14. Be righteous, be self-aggrandizing. 15. Write the worst poem in the world. 16. Show up even though you don't know what to say. 17. Watch television when you want to write. Write when you want to watch television. 18. Make messes. 19. Bake. 20. Listen to Ani DiFranco on the scratchy CD you played the summer you lived alone in Provincetown and drove to the sunset every night. Remember the canopy of trees, sand in the road, people on bicycles with picnic baskets strapped to their backs. 21. Remember how it felt to be at the beginning, alone, your desires almost unbearable, how you kept trying to contain them, and they kept showing you where you needed to go.

Poem That Gives No Fucks

A poem should be heavy metal

worn as armor when the world hurts.

Should be a jangly guitar arpeggio

draping the highway or blue jay pecking apart

a robin's egg, crisp blue fragments split with red.

A poem should be a Lisa Frank unicorn

vomiting rainbows who makes you ask:

how do I continue to do what I hate

day in and day out, and then answers

"Bitch, one day you're going to grow wings

so stop screaming into the 22nd century.

Get nasty, mechanize the messy.

Reinvent your pussy into a box of butterflies."

Because if a poem isn't god's tooth

tonguing you for gold then it's only a half moonwalk,

only a date with the toilet and last night's chardonnay.

A poem should feel like an encyclopedia

chewed up by stray dogs behind a Tiger Mart.

Seductive as a saint with truck driver hands.

Should glint like a prayer made of bodily fluids,

make you want to burn all your clothes,

eat yourself alive, smother your heart

and say: I've been searching

for the blues my whole damn life.

*Ode to Vaginal Tearing Disguised as Fan Mail
to Courtney Love*

Flurry of raccoons cutting

Britney Spears' silhouette in an alleyway

Music box with one bruised

Dancer convulsing inside

I don't want to say you're cynical

As a Trustafarian screaming "sell out"

Outside an H&M

Or that you're insufferable

As a college student who read

The Metamorphoses and believes

They were once a comb, barnacle

Snail tattoo on a lover's wrist

But when the midwife's hands trace the V

Where I fail to heal

Crooked and backlit as a pinball machine

Or cylinder of discontinued energy drink

Shining on the floor of a rest stop

When she eats her Lean Cuisine and tells me

She can reset the flesh

With mercury and I will be symmetrical again

Although the oceanic ledge

Of skin will burn for weeks

I think praise the damage

The botched job

Of lidocaine and stitches

As I held my baby

Pulsing with adrenaline

For the first time not feeling

Where the skin tore

Under a bright and uneven glare

Ebullient as a bivalve crusted with stars

Cracked open and uncouth

The way I've always wanted to be:

Throbbing at the bottom of a tank like a lobster

Not caring how I might come back up

Ode to Slug Disguised as Letter to a Men's Rights Activist

I imagine we both like burritos

and enjoy sitting for long stretches

at a desk half-heartedly searching

through the forested backlogs

of Pornhub to relish the chafe

and exhale of deliverance. Or how

I sometimes get aroused

via humiliation. Or shame.

Or the very thought

that I am a sexual being

and my desire is folded

up inside of me like a wet

envelope. But I hope that's where

we part ways, as the slug

parts from its semenlike

trail, and shall we consider,

for a moment, the slug, whose inscription

of swampy air and brittle

light purchases a particular

parcel of disgust in my chest;

little cavity of unnameable

ooze pilfered with a thwack

on hot summer days—

the only living thing I felt entitled

to hurt—not kill—as a child

(although I'd stomp

whole amphitheaters of ants

in the heat-sueded dirt.) Yes I wanted

to hurt them, for the very fact

I thought they couldn't feel—

their surplus of congealed

dew, alienlike snot. Holy cum.

Yes. That coveted and bloated

with mystery. I wanted to know

what engine gurgled inside

like a melted gear, the sun's hooked

cock. To find the seam in their seamless

body. Maybe that's what it's like

to feel so entitled to something

as when I look at the moon-

soaked sky, pearled and

apostrophed with clouds

and know that my heart

and lungs will eventually unravel

like cashmere in a moth's spangled maw

receding just when I want it most.

On the Cusp of 36 I Remember the Only Republican at My College Gave Me Head and I Didn't Come

1. not because a mediocre hippy band
leaked from cheap speakers

2. the kind of record you play
when you want to seduce someone

3. but you're also in a hurry
and a bit lazy

4. not because I wasn't into muscles
or his politics which were vague

5. and uninformed like a precursor
to Jordan Peterson subreddits

6. or the funk of loneliness
that pervaded the room

7. his and my own dappled scent
clanging together which is not the same

8. as solitude but the ways we try to escape it;
going home with someone because

9. they are strong enough to flip you
over their shoulders like a prize

10. I was sober and 19 and carried Valium
in an Altoids case my mother gave me

11. after my first panic attack
where my heart flapped against

12. itself and I never felt cozier
than that night

13. swaddled in my childhood bed
the drug pinning me to the earth

14. pleasure not an escape
but an anchoring of the self

15. a bearing down and lifting
out of the fizzled murk

16. he twirled his shirt above his head and went in
for the plunge and I felt nothing

17. I am writing this poem on my phone
at the airport waiting for a delayed flight

18. listening to Lou Reed sing "Here She Comes Now"
like music to a funeral procession

19. taking in the verdict we knew was inevitable
and I can't stomach the kindness

20. in his voice or the finality of him
being gone and maybe it was fatigue

21. maybe I'd had enough
pleasure that day and wanted only

22. to be close to a body
to have someone hold me down

23. to be hummed toward uncertainty
like a half-made resolution

24. praising what is messy and obvious

25. that he didn't ask for anything in return

26. that his chin was raw

27. that I kissed the cleft where it gleamed

28. that I walked back to my dorm

29. and didn't care who saw

30. that I did a heel-kick midair

31. like Fred Astaire's spirit

32. gilding my cheek

33. that I danced in the cold

34. my whole self lovely and stained

35. shimmering with fluids

36. entirely my own

I Was 35 and Driving Route 40 When I Understood Why My Mother Escaped

into her private room of grief
whenever "Piece of My Heart" came on the radio
& she would close her eyes like clasping shut
a clutch of tobacco & enter the gauzy
lounge in which Janice bloomed
her mantel of feathers & voltage
steering the car as if into the cleavage
of song as it broke & slipped
around her shoulders as she sang
the way women do who think the blues
is a lifetime of silence giving them
permission to scream into the plum-fuck
ether belting "Take It"
the notes shedding like molted velvet
& I watched her lean
into its edge thinking
it was heartache or the blur
of love nudging her forward
not what I see now
switching lanes two exits
from the street where I will turn off
the car radio & fold my desires
into the glove compartment
where I once kept a stack of vellum
to make my body loose
as a hum spooled out in voluptuous rings
that my mother wasn't
mourning men who'd left
or broken her heart
but the sweetness of oblivion
slashing an empty room
with that final wail
how it is not like breaking at all.

I Hope Hillary Is Having Good Sex

I hope Hillary is having good sex

I say to myself at the farmers' market

While fingering the over-ripened bustier

Of an heirloom tomato

So close to rot it nearly sucks

My pinky into its dappled maw

I hope she's at least getting decent head I say again

Now that she's proven a woman

Can win the popular vote

And still lose to an imbecile

Because sexism

Because Russian interference

Because my grandmother

Who worked for LBJ and then

Nixon and was harassed by male coworkers

Until she had to quit

Even she said of Hillary, "There is something

About that woman I just don't trust"

I hope Hillary is getting it in

By Bill or someone better at listening

Who asks her what she needs

Then gets directly down to business

Without preamble or pussyfooting

Someone who emerges

Only for a sandwich or breath of fresh air

I hope she has multiple sidepieces

Each a different build and scent

And when they ask

To see her closet full of immaculate suits

Organized and shimmering on their racks

Like a god's molted skin

She lets them touch just the hem

Thinking About How I Never Say the Word Cunt

Even though it fits neatly on the tongue

Like a penny or compressed tab of Diet Coke

Even though it is the kryptonite of syphilitic dictators

But never fiendish poets or burnt out actors

Callused invective of the heart

Stammering like a fleet of frat boys' loafered hooves

Thinking of Richard Burton

Who described Elizabeth Taylor's

Asshole with such tenderness

As if it were an injured fawn, tended to it

When it became infected

Enchanted by its geography and hymns

And learned to call it by its thousand balmy names

But never once uttered a syllable about her immaculate cunt

As in dream thief, spell

To protect what I love

As in tic I will acquire

When I am old and tired of holding the demons in

I will stutter *Cunt Cunt Cunt*

On the bright carriage of my unraveling

The word a sip, infusion

Safety valve, a reckoning

Palm of nickels clicked into a payphone

Mouthful of smoke blistering the air

"I Want to Burn the Frat House of America to the Ground"

I have seen the white columned porches

from which insignias blare

across lawns shimmering like art installations

made from tailgate chairs

and solo cups where I'd hold

my breath until I reached the end of frat row

eclipsed by khaki legs spread boldly

as the tilt of a student's confidently

capped head under which a smirk gleamed

"I am the one paying you to be here"

by which I mean this poem could be titled

my mother tells me her #MeToo stories

I mean I have never felt

at home inside myself

after my daughter was born

I washed my hands and counted

breaths, synapses of light

blinking messages

in the hollows of my bones

like a purging of joy

by which I mean my hands

became so clean I couldn't feel

my child as she slept

in my arms

by which I mean my mother held me

and she didn't

I mean my mother's body was a house burning

and I've been burning ever since

Neruda, Maybe You Are the Reason Why

I sat watching mackerel

pierce the surface of the Pacific

like the moon's studded harbors

jeweled and empty

why I lived hazardously

with a family who praised

Pinochet around the corner from

a wholesale store where I was taken

to buy birth control

pills one morning

by their son who held me

down and told me to swallow

all of them at once after which

I bled for days

hitchhiked through the Andes

and tasted its green heart

pulling one word into another

as if from the center of a glacier

unraveling with bruised glee

Neruda, I've made peace with it:

your poems couldn't save you

but eventually they saved me.

Seville

Because the cathedral leaked yellow light

onto cobblestones like a slit carton of milk.

Because boxes of red wine emptied

down the throat's swiveling street.

Because the music of my footsteps

like notes of ash.

Because he curved like a question mark

puncturing a flap of heaven.

Because *litros* tucked in brown paper bags.

two packs of Chesterfields a day,

at the breakfast table,

on the lip of a balcony.

Because I woke in a shrine

of my own stickiness.

Because his lips were aperitif.

Because my father kissed his forehead

outside the mosque,

the taste of rum and rose petals.

Because oranges bulging in coat pockets.

Because the condom held against the light,

swirling cities of children we would never conceive.

Because it broke,

the cartography of longing pulsed onto soft thigh.

Because the long walk home chaperoned by stray dogs,

the drunk's grief of the Guadalquivir,

blue cough and jasmine rotting in my hair.

Because I passed out in the bar bathroom

and mistook the toilet for my mother's legs.

Because the shard of glass in the singer's throat.

Because he cried when he was happy.

Because the thief looked me in the eyes and didn't take the purse.

Because the petroglyphs of our hands wounded the white walls,

how we made the world small,

siphoning god's breath

to sweeten the blood-flavored noon.

I Was in Love with a City

before I loved the skin and blood
that makes me human, coupling of ghosts

and sky. I was in love with the litanies
of doves crashing against cathedrals

in love with the ejaculation of jeweled alphabets
streaking into a reckless night

in love with the word
for residence and loneliness and orchestrations of dusk

in love with the violin strapped to a motorcyclist's back
weaving through traffic

the delicate maneuverings required of us
to be in this world

in love with
the sea's hubris

the banter of silk
and premonitions washed ashore each morning

the seagull's labor
of pulling one thing apart from itself

leaving the beach a bruised mosaic
in love with residues of elegance

godly remnants of glass
an urchin's bloomed configuration

its tongue a bell
its tongue a dictionary

where every word is *more*
valve and soot

looted museum
may we all return to such

opacity and salt
all impulse and libido and albumen

sent out from the body threaded
and translucent as prayer

I Don't Like to Have Sex While I'm on My Period

even though my husband is the kind of guy

who isn't afraid

of a woman's fluids

who might even go down

if the flow is light

a real man

you might say

if the logic wasn't steeped

in toxic masculinity the way

the sheets are steeped in blood

after making love on day three

the rasp of stain beneath us

like a bat fluttering its wings

in a puddle of Robitussin

I can't help but think

it's crude

to put down a towel

before we begin

the way a man sticks a gloved

finger up his wife's vagina

to assess if she's done bleeding

clean you might say

if that language wasn't steeped

in violent misogyny

because isn't my blood the cleanest

part about me

fuck a towel

if you want to go deep

you better be willing to draw blood

my husband is a real man

isn't afraid to smell

the shed lining

muffle his face in the spasm of cells

wasn't afraid to watch our daughter

emerge and split me open

crowning

which means my body

concussed around her like a crown

which means

there was so much blood

I had to touch it

to remember where I came from

the hot and pulsing corona

ruckus of DNA

metallic and stinging

Love, forgive me

I do not want to be touched

while my body

orchestrates this unraveling

as much as I love

the bouquet of clots

rioting around the base of your cock

bright as a truck stop souvenir

to own a part of you

where the blood remains

dried

and hissing

a dwelling

of dank perfume

as the body

travels back to its source

and I am answerable to no one

not even my own name

I Don't Think Neruda Was Thinking of My Tampon

when he wrote
"Body of a Woman"
how it bloats and swells
with urine every time I pee
or the diva cup I consider buying
in the health food store while
Paganini's First Concerto for Violin
pierces through my ear buds
with arpeggios I first heard
on the car radio when I was 17
and the music inked into me
its gauzy ambition
I choose Size Two
"for women over thirty who've given birth"
which is a polite way
of saying LOOSE
but tonight I'm feeling romantic
thoughtfully tearing
into a package
of cherry pie
in my parked Subaru
and imagine what it might
feel like to be rendered
under the glow
of the CITGO sign
which is so much like the moon
I can't tell the difference
There was the lover
who said my body was
as good as Drew Barrymore's
another who said I was better
looking naked than he predicted
and another who said

I looked like a child
and prostitute combined
and the one who hissed
I was so beautiful
it made him want to hurt me
Is this what you meant, Neruda
when you wrote *you stretch out*
like the world
the jetty of curls
that thickens with blood
on the last day of my period
Did you mean
the shimmer and molt
the near-death stink
of a movie theater's
overflowing dark as the credits
unfurl and entrails
of crushed candy
scribble over the plush carpet
or a banquet hall flashing
with half-filled BINGO cards
or the IHOP sign off Storrow Drive
like a church marquee
announcing I'm almost home
Did you mean rows
of Slim Jims
gleaming in their packages
of synthetic skin
a beard of neon dust
sprawling across my chin
hunched in the dark
of a gas station bathroom
where the attendant
keeps vanilla scented air freshener
plugged into the wall
could you have imagined me

pulling a cup of blood
from my body and if so
was there a word you felt
and was it envy

I Could Write a Poem About Electric Scooters

the ones self-described disruptors
created and left scattered

in the touristy districts
of Nashville— which is to say white—

which is to say I don't know
how to travel and not be grotesque

as the blonde bachelorette parties
on their booze wagons that leave me breathless—

the desire to sprawl and develop
just like Jesus himself who must have said

thou shalt fuck
over thy neighbor if it makes a profit—

I could write the scooters are lime green
and today I saw a woman riding one

in a tattered wedding dress
she found at Goodwill—the kind of slip

I was never tough enough to wear
but envied the girls who could, the ones

who channeled Kathleen Hanna
and Courtney Love and gave

blow jobs behind the bleachers—Oh
to be at home like that in my own body—

to be in the world like a tech
entrepreneur and possess so little

consideration for the world
I can glide right through it

like the frat boy who bought
the historical home next door

and turned it into a bicycle shop
who also drives a red pickup

with a sticker of an AR-15 that says
"come and take it"

which is another way of saying
"who's going to stop me"

which is the smirk of Kavanaugh
which is the smirk of every man

who's been stockpiling
alibis since he was 17—

thou shall not—
fuck sustainability

I want to be the girl
burning down this street at rush hour,

dress like the iridescence
of an oil-soaked wing—

"come and get this pussy"
written on her forehead

in blood
ready to take down

the motherfucker
who tries to grab her next.

#Team Rat

God bless the back issues
Of *Vanity Fair* & *Good Housekeeping*

Whose pages I gloss
In the dentist's waiting room

Like *Playboys* for chocolate cake
Recipes that include mayonnaise

& a fashion shoot where the model
Levitates in the aurora-blue

Ovum of a feeling I can't describe
But know like "Autumn Leaves"

Throbbing in a strip mall's
Sound system. God bless

The retired nurse
Sitting across from me

In her floral bomber
Who types on her phone

With the sound on
So I can hear each letter

Tingle under her index
Like an otter

Clacking clamshells
Between its paws.

God bless the otter
And its abundance

Of memes
Mirroring 21st century

Desperation
For something decent

To flash across our screens
Even if it's a fraudulent video

Of a dog rescuing a goat
Or a pig overturning a turtle

& maybe I'm projecting
But I prefer the rat

Dragging its festering purse
Of pizza down subway steps

Like Fred Astaire
Gliding on gilded hooves

I prefer the possum
& its febrile coat

Of scab and moonshine
How it looks mid-

Shriek in every picture
Baring teeth

Like it might shred
The hand that tries

To rescue her
But doesn't

& I've read that if you find
A possum killed by a car

You should look
Inside the womb

Reach your hand
Into the gummy guts

The way I reached into
My own darkness

To touch my baby
As she emerged

Marveling at the animal
In me that would have

Torn myself open
I say god bless

Anyone willing to kneel
Beside a body

& conjure resurrection
From the muck

Of starlessness and decay
The tingle of tiny breaths

Piercing through the night
The way my daughter

Seemed to sing her name
As she entered the world

Announcing herself
Again and again.

Isn't 'Food Court' a Lovely Term

not just the sound but the place

I mean aren't Panda Express and Sbarros lovely

with their food garnished on metal trays

how when I'm inside of one

I feel home no matter how far

up Route 65 between Kentucky and Indiana

where churches and Subway franchises

neck and I know exactly where I must go

to reach the good Starbucks and avoid the McDonald's

where high school students hand out gift cards

"From Jesus because he loves you"

and I almost took one once

I had been driving alone for hours

on my way to a conference

where I would have gotten drunk

in the good old days

would have gotten tanked

and made some bad decision

not out of stupidity or self-destruction

but a deliberate attempt

to feel more than I thought

the world has to offer

like ransacking a hotel's free buffet

stuffing my pockets full

of food I'll never eat

I didn't yet understand

the beauty of a road

connecting towns I'll never see in daylight

decked out in neon effigies

each vestibule offering its own flavor

of sanctuary

or I did

and couldn't tolerate it

how I took the gift card

from the girl's hand

and imagined what it would feel like

to be forgiven

and for a moment I was

and I gave it back

I Am Not Trying to Hide My Hungers
from the World Anymore

Not trying to wipe the smears
of gold from my chin

not trying to erase the decadence
of seeds and profanity

of grease not trying
to pretend I don't open

my mouth around the zaftig
pearls of rain in the middle

of the night or that I don't love
the moment right before sleep

when I am most tender
and translucent my bladder half-filled

knowing I will have to get up
and pee knowing my daughter

will wake up before I am ready
the way I became aware of her

on a climb through the mountains
a heaviness in my limbs a gentle

premonition as I walked later
to the Rite Aid and knew in my hands

and I knew in my mouth
and I knew in the way my body

pulled me forward as I wept
with joy but also grief

that a part of my life was ending
and isn't it good to know when

life is about to swallow you whole
take you in its arms and say

"Live, bitch, live"
and you believe it

and this is how I will carry her
from her crib and open the curtains

partway not ready to let the
world in the trails of smoke

and exhaust winter-blue
as Cat Stevens' *Mona Bone Jakon*

spinning on the Crosley
that opens like an old suitcase

when my daughter stands
on a chair lifting the stylus

from its perch guiding
it to the starry chatter

that hisses between songs
wondering what will play next

There Is a Moment I Feel Free

driving to the taco place
where a few weeks back

a shooting happened
right where our car was parked

and in retrospect
it seems negligent

to have been that happy
sitting at the counter

squeezing limes
over everything

and Aretha
is now in my speakers

the song where she sings
in quick succession

"you're all I need to get by . . .
baby you know that you got me"

and maybe motherhood
has made me soft

which is close to a kind
of ghoulishness

I don't know
I know it has taken me

35 years to learn how to dress
appropriately for the weather

to apply moisturizer before bed
and sunscreen in the morning

to be this in love
with the life I've made

and care for it
no matter how reckless that is

Crow Flying Overhead with a Hole in Its Wing

I looked up and saw you this morning

flying over a Tex-Mex restaurant

the hole in your wing

the size of a bottle cap

I googled what it means

and read about parasites

but nothing about whether it is

a benediction

to see an animal flying

with this perfect portal in its wing

through which I saw the sky

through which its jeweled language

leaked muted and streaky

through which I heard

the first song I ever played my daughter

holding her near the window

that overlooks our street

through which I saw everything

I had been afraid of

which was a kind of death

which was a kind of

abandon

buckling toward joy

as I have fallen to my knees

in grief

but have never known

what it sounds like

to sing without expecting

mercy

through which the wind

might touch us

which is the only

benediction I need

Notes

The book's epigraph is from Julio Cortázar's "A Love Letter/Una Carta de Amor" published in *Twilight: Selected Poems* (City Lights Books) translated by Stephen Kessler.

The last line of "I Pump Milk like a Boss" is in conversation with Maggie Smith's poem "Invincible."

In "Love Letter with The Beatles, Lana Del Rey, and Julio Cortázar" the second to last stanza's italicized lines are from Julio Cortázar's "A Love Letter/Una Carta de Amor" published in *Twilight: Selected Poems* (City Lights Books) translated by Stephen Kessler.

"Poem That Gives No Fucks" is composed of lines written by students who participated in my workshop "Irreverent Joy: Writing the Poem That Gives No Fucks" at Third Man Records in 2017.

"On the Cusp of 36 I Remember the Only Republican at My College Gave Me Head and I Didn't Come" refers to the Kavanaugh hearing in which Christine Blasey Ford heroically testified.

"'I Want to Burn the Frat House of America to the Ground'" takes its title from Jennifer Weiner's op-ed "The Patriarchy Will Always Have Its Revenge," *The New York Times*, September 28, 2018.

Many of these poems are indebted to the work of writers published in *MUTHA Magazine* and *Revolutionary Mothering: Love on the Front Lines*, as well as talks by Aracelis Girmay and Rachel McKibbens at the 2016 AWP Conference in Washington, DC.

Acknowledgments

Deepest gratitude to the editors and readers of the following journals in which these poems first appeared, at times in earlier versions:

The Academy of American Poets Poem-a-Day: "Seville," a section of "Love Letter with The Beatles, Lana Del Rey, and Julio Cortázar";

The Account: "Isn't 'Food Court' a Lovely Term," "I Hope Hillary Is Having Good Sex," "I Don't Like to Have Sex While I'm on My Period," "There Is a Moment I Feel Free," "Crow Flying Overhead with a Hole in Its Wing";

American Poetry Review: "I Am Not Trying to Hide My Hungers from the World Anymore";

Columbia Journal: "Why in Some Hospitals They Don't Let You Hold Hands During Labor," "Love Letter with The Beatles, Lana Del Rey, and Julio Cortázar," "Ode to Vaginal Tearing Disguised as Fan Mail to Courtney Love," "I Don't Think Neruda Was Thinking of My Tampon";

Four Way Review: "I Could Write a Poem About Electric Scooters";

Great River Review: "On the Cusp of 36 I Remember the Only Republican at My College Gave Me Head and I Didn't Come," "I Was 35 and Driving Route 40 When I Understood Why My Mother Escaped," "Thinking About How I Never Say the Word *Cunt*," "I Was in Love with a City";

Los Angeles Review: "I Pump Milk like a Boss," "I Write Poems About Motherhood";

Pangyrus: "Ode to Slug Disguised as Letter to a Men's Rights Activist";

Poets.org: "Weaning, I Listen to Paganini's Concerto No. 1";

Queerpoets: "I Would Like to Tell the President to Eat a Dick in a Non-Homophobic Way" (with Greek translation);

Tin House Magazine: "Self-Portrait as Getting Drunk-Dialed by God," "Weaning, I Listen to Tyler, the Creator," "Weaning, I Listen to Paganini's Concerto No. 1";

Waxwing: "I Would Like to Tell the President to Eat a Dick in a Non-Homophobic Way," "Love Poem in the Style of Jordan's Furniture," "I Am Thinking About the Movie *Con Air*."

"I Pump Milk like a Boss" is also included in *Best of Los Angeles Review, 2018* and *The Long Devotion: Poets Writing Motherhood*.

This book would not be possible without the support of the National Endowment for the Arts. Thank you to the NEA staff and Katy Day.

Love and gratitude to my poetry family for your brilliance and heart: Wendy Chin-Tanner, Tiana Clark, Allison Inman, Katie Greene, Derrick Harriell, Steve Haruch, Susanna Kwan, Jennifer and Keith Leonard, Galen Malicoat, Tyler Mills, José Olivarez, Lindsey Rome, Maggie Smith, Mikah Wyman Stuible, Elizabeth Townsend, and the Nashville poetry community. Thank you Kazim Ali, Paul Guest, Keetje Kuipers, and Adrian Matejka for your inspiration and support. Thank you Ciona Rouse—these poems bloomed at the edges of our conversations and dreams. Thank you Jeffrey McDaniel, my first and forever poetry coach.

Special and deepest thanks to Julie Aaron and Boo Gordon. I am grateful for your light, warmth, and wisdom. This book would not exist without your care.

Thank you to my students and friends at The Hugo House, Sarah Lawrence College, Split This Rock, Third Man Books, and Vanderbilt University. Thank you Kim Baugh, Siobhan Boroian, Ben Swank, Chet Weise, and the Third Man Records family. Thank you to bookstore owners and booksellers everywhere, especially Joelle Herr at The Bookshop.

Thank you Katherine Bradford for the incredible cover art and for your generosity, and many thanks to the Portland Museum of Art for this contribution.

Thank you Hanif Abdurraqib, Ross Gay, and Michelle Tea for your words that grace this book and for your work that lights the way.

Thank you Eloisa Amezcua for reading the manuscript in its earlier version and pushing it forward with your smart, generous feedback. Thank you Erika Meitner and Camille Dungy for seeing this book, and for your mentorship and friendship.

Gratitude to my BOA family, especially Peter Conners, Sandy Knight, and Ron Martin-Dent for your support and vision in bringing this book into the world.

Thank you to my family: Pamela and Ted DeColo, Sophia Snell, Keith Stubbs, Molly Hockman, the Korine family, Haywood Berman, Liz Santiago, and Molly Siegel.

To the women who guarded the doors while I pumped milk and wrote poems. Thank you.

For Avi, my sweetheart and best friend, you make everything possible. I love you.

For my daughter, the heart underneath my heart. I am so lucky I get to be your mama.

And for Miriam Margolies Stubbs who saw the poet in me and gave her a home.

About the Author

Kendra DeColo was born in Boston and spent much of her child-hood in Provincetown, Massachusetts. She is the author of *My Dinner with Ron Jeremy* (Third Man Books, 2016) and *Thieves in the Afterlife* (Saturnalia Books, 2014), selected by Yusef Komunyakaa for the 2013 Saturnalia Books Poetry Prize. She has received awards and fellowships from the National Endowment for the Arts, MacDowell, the Bread Loaf Writers' Conference, the Millay Colony, Split This Rock, and the Tennessee Arts Commission. Her poems and essays have appeared in *American Poetry Review, Tin House Magazine, Waxwing, Los Angeles Review, Bitch Magazine, VIDA,* and elsewhere. She has performed her work in comedy clubs and music venues including the Newport Folk Festival, and she has taught at Sarah Lawrence College, Vanderbilt University, and the Tennessee Prison for Women. She currently teaches at The Hugo House and lives with her family in Nashville, Tennessee.

BOA Editions, Ltd.
American Poets Continuum Series

Colophon

BOA Editions, Ltd., a not-for-profit publisher of poetry and other literary works, fosters readership and appreciation of contemporary literature. By identifying, cultivating, and publishing both new and established poets and selecting authors of unique literary talent, BOA brings high-quality literature to the public.

Support for this effort comes from the sale of its publications, grant funding, and private donations.

The publication of this book is made possible, in part, by the special support of the following individuals:

Anonymous (x2)
Anya Backlund, Blue Flower Arts
Angela Bonazinga & Catherine Lewis
Gary & Gwen Conners
The Chris Dahl & Ruth Rowse Charitable Fund
The David J. Fraher Charitable Fund, *in memory of A. Poulin, Jr.*
Margaret Heminway
Kathleen C. Holcombe
Nora A. Jones
Keetje & Sarah Kuipers
Paul LaFerriere & Dorrie Parini
John & Barbara Lovenheim
Joe McElveney
Boo Poulin
Deborah Ronnen
Thomas Smith & Louise Spinelli
Elizabeth Spenst
David St. John
William Waddel & Linda Rubel
Michael Waters & Mihaela Moscaliuc

CPSIA information can be obtained
at www.ICGtesting.com
Printed in the USA
BVHW031124140421
604840BV00010B/19